Who comes first?

Who comes first?

Inspiring stories from the history of the Games

Chris Hudson

Barnabas
in
Schools

Barnabas for Children® is a registered word mark and the logo is a registered device mark of
The Bible Reading Fellowship

Text copyright © Chris Hudson 2011
Illustrations copyright © Simon Smith 2011
The author asserts the moral right
to be identified as the author of this work

Published by
The Bible Reading Fellowship
15 The Chambers, Vineyard
Abingdon OX14 3FE
United Kingdom
Tel: +44 (0)1865 319700
Email: enquiries@brf.org.uk
Website: www.brf.org.uk
BRF is a Registered Charity

ISBN 978 0 85746 048 6
First published 2011
10 9 8 7 6 5 4 3 2 1 0
All rights reserved

Acknowledgments
Unless otherwise stated, scripture quotations are taken from the Contemporary English Version of
the Bible published by HarperCollins Publishers, copyright © 1991, 1992, 1995
American Bible Society.

A catalogue record for this book is available from the British Library

Printed in Singapore by Craft Print International Ltd

The paper used in the production of this publication was supplied
by mills that source their raw materials from sustainably managed forests.
Soy-based inks were used in its printing and the laminate film is biodegradable.

Contents

Introduction

Does sport have anything of value to teach us?

The Olympic and Paralympic Games aim to celebrate Respect, Excellence, Friendship, Courage, Determination, Inspiration and Equality. Indeed, Pierre de Coubertin (founder of the 'revived' modern Games) believed they would foster world peace:

> May joy and good fellowship reign, and in this manner, may the Olympic Torch pursue its way through ages, increasing friendly understanding among nations, for the good of a humanity always more enthusiastic, more courageous and more pure.

Was he being slightly naive? The Ancient Greek Games could be ultra-violent and highly nationalistic. Events such as the Panakriton (a form of extreme wrestling) were brutal and occasionally fatal, and many of the events were simply the display of battlefield skills under competition rules. Wars weren't necessarily cancelled during Olympic years (as they were meant to be), women and slaves were banned from competing, some teams were refused entry, and many Greek cities used the event to intimidate their rivals. In the twentieth century, the modern Games have witnessed terrorism (Munich 1972), extreme nationalism (Berlin 1936 and others), the settling of 'old scores' (the 1956 Russia/Hungary water polo final), political protests or boycotts (Moscow 1980 and many others) and the use of illegal performance-enhancing drugs and other treatments (East Germany's team in the 1970s and 1980s, and others).

And yet... there is still something marvellous when we see a well-won victory by a skilled athlete working at the peak of their fitness. Sporting competitions can promote so many positive messages about discipline, dedication and determination. There are rules to follow, team members to encourage, and supporters to lift your spirits and cheer you on. Could that inspire our own pupils? A lot of schools are banking on it, and hopefully yours will too.

This resource is intended to help you explore Olympic and Paralympic values with your pupils in Religious Education, PSE, Citizenship and Literacy lessons, assemblies and Collective Worship. Elsewhere, there'll be lots of advice for celebrating the Games in primary school, with excellent opportunities for cross-curricular work in Literacy, Numeracy, Science, Art, Geography, History... so why use Religious Education and Collective Worship as well?

Think back to your own schooldays, and the way sport was used to reinforce school values. My own (admittedly rather negative) experiences from school sports suggest that PE can sometimes be part of an unconscious 'hidden curriculum' celebrating values that talk about certain sorts of people being intrinsically 'better' than others. This resource aims to counter that by encouraging children to ask hard questions about 'sporting values', to respond to true-life stories in a variety of ways—and reflect positively on what this all has to do with them.

How to use this book

The suggested lesson plans and activities will need to be adapted by you to suit the different aptitudes and abilities in your class. There is a mix of suggested activities to accompany each story—but in RE lessons, always try to relate the pupil activities to your RE objectives, which means including *at least* one of the suggested RE pupil activities in the lesson. Of course, a cross-curricular approach will allow you to tick a lot of other subject 'boxes', and allow you to approach the same topic from a variety of angles with a variety of approaches—but please don't sacrifice the RE.

This book approaches the topic from a broadly Christian perspective, but others will have insights too. Hopefully, the lesson material will get your class talking about their own values, and generate discussion across different faiths and beliefs—and as the class teacher, you may want to add other stories and ideas from other traditions, using the model presented here. The key message, like that for the Games, is probably... Enjoy!

The suggested websites are useful resources, but they can be subject to change—so teachers should always check the current state of a website for suitability before sending children towards it for research purposes.

Who Comes First?

... is also available as a Barnabas RE Day of story-telling, role-play, drama and games, exploring the connections between faith, belief, personal motivation and physical education. It's been put together especially with a view to complementing cross-curricular work on the Games—and it could come to your primary school during 2012. Book early to avoid disappointment!

For more details see www.barnabasinschools.org.uk
Or phone: 01865 319700

Stories
and lesson material

Respect

1960

Wilma Rudolph

Respect

Wilma Rudolph

Sprinter, 100m and 200m (Rome 1960)

'The triumph can't be had without the struggle. And I know what struggle is. I have spent a lifetime trying to share what it has meant to be a woman first in the world of sports, so that other young women have a chance to reach their dreams.'

Wilma Rudolph

As a child, Wilma was always getting sick. Her family were poor, but although there was never enough money, she always felt loved and cared for. However, they couldn't afford a doctor. So when Wilma contracted polio (a disease that wastes away your leg muscles) the only doctor in town who would treat her said she would never walk again. Wilma's mother didn't agree. There was a university hospital 50 miles away that she knew would treat her child—so twice a week, for two years, Wilma was taken there for physiotherapy. She had to walk with a crutch, wear a metal brace on one leg and corrective shoes on both feet just to walk straight. Her family were taught how to exercise Wilma at home as well, and they did it, brothers and sisters too. So, by the age of twelve, Wilma didn't need that kind of help anymore. She had recovered. And now she wanted to run.

At high school, she made the basketball team, and also practised hard at a local running track. After being spotted by a local coach, she was soon competing and winning at the state athletic championships. By 1956, she was part of the USA's team in the 4x100m relay, and took home a bronze medal for it—and the 1960 Rome Games saw her take three gold medals for the 100m, 200m and 4x100m relay. She was now breaking athletic records set by men, and going further. Wilma then represented her country at other athletics meetings around the world—and kept on winning in competition after competition. All of a sudden she was famous! The US president invited her to see him at the White House, and there were further parades to join and awards to win as she travelled the world. It was all very new and exciting for a young woman.

But then one day, an invitation to a special event made her stop and think very hard. Wilma's own childhood town of Clarksville had invited her back for a civic reception to celebrate her achievements. There would be music, speeches and thousands of people attending. But it would be 'segregated', as everything was in Clarksville. At that time, parts of the USA practised 'segregation', where people of different races were kept apart as much as possible. Segregation meant that Wilma had to ride at the back of the bus, could only go to school with other black children and was only ever seen by a black doctor. And the civic reception to celebrate her gold medal performances would be segregated too. Wilma thought very hard; then she put her foot down—and said 'No.' What? No.

She *wouldn't* come to a civic reception in her home town that was segregated. If the races couldn't mix freely there, then she wouldn't go. It was a powerful decision. The city council had to think very hard too—but they couldn't ignore her. So finally they gave in. The big day came—and 40,000 local people of all races and backgrounds turned up to cheer their sporting heroine, together. It was a brilliant moment—and afterwards, Wilma said it was one of the best things she ever did.

Activities

Lesson plan
Introduction

Ask pupils to discuss in pairs what their proudest moment has ever been, and ask a few to share it with the class.

Read aloud Wilma's story. Afterwards emphasise the following key points:

- Wilma (with her family) had to work hard to overcome her childhood polio, because black people then usually had a much lower income, and they were not allowed to use the same doctors and hospitals in Clarksville as white people.
- 'Segregation' is not legal now in the USA because of a strong campaign led by Dr Martin Luther King and other people like Wilma Rudolph.
- Their campaign was peaceful and non-violent, based on the teachings both of Mohandas Gandhi and the biblical life and words of Jesus of Nazareth.
- Wilma was a devout Baptist Christian whose faith expressed itself in a desire for racial justice, in the same way that it later led her to support the work of evangelists such as Dr Billy Graham.

Pupil activities

Religious Education

1. Segregation in the USA was finally defeated after a long campaign by African-American churches like the one Wilma attended. Read the following Bible passages. Which of these do you think would have most influenced Wilma to take a stand against segregation? Put the letter of the most important at the top, the next two in the middle, and the least important at the bottom. Explain your choice.

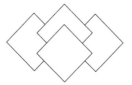

(a) 'I give you peace, the kind of peace that only I can give. It isn't like the peace that this world can give. So don't be worried or afraid.' John 14:27

17

(b) 'If you have faith when you pray, you will be given whatever you ask for.' Matthew 21:22

(c) 'Faith in Christ Jesus makes each of you equal with each other, whether you are a Jew or a Greek, a slave or a free person, a man or a woman.' Galatians 3:28

(d) 'I tell you not to try and get even with a person who has done something bad to you.' Matthew 5:39

(e) 'We often suffer, but we are never crushed. Even when we don't know what to do, we never give up. In times of trouble, God is with us, and when we are knocked down, we get up again.' 2 Corinthians 4:8–9

2. Wilma used her talents and skills to make a difference. If you have talents and skills, what responsibilities do you have to use them? Jesus once said to his followers, 'You are the light of the world. A city on a hill cannot be hidden. Neither do people light a lamp and put it under a bowl. Instead, they put it on its stand, and it gives light to everyone in the house. In the same way, let your light shine before other people, that they may see your good deeds and praise your Father in Heaven' (Matthew 5:14–16). In the middle of a page, draw a candle or an Olympic flame with your name on it. Nearby, show rays of light flying away from it. What skills or talents do you have that could help make the world a 'brighter', kinder and more fair place? Write them or draw them on the rays of light. What would be a good title for this?

PSE, Citizenship, Literacy

1. We can use the word respect to mean all sorts of things. With a partner, try to come up with three sentences that use the word to mean different things. Then try to create a dictionary definition that lists all the possible meanings of the word, and write it out. Now consult a printed dictionary, and copy out its definition. In what ways are your definitions similar, and different? What do you think Wilma's story has to say about respect? Draw the five

connected rings that make up the Olympic flag, and inside the rings write five words that you think are needed to create a world where everyone shows respect to each other.

2. Read these comments from Wilma Rudolph.

    'When I was going through my transition of being famous, I tried to ask God why was I here? What was my purpose? Surely, it wasn't just to win three gold medals. There has to be more to this life than that.'

    'What do you do after you are world famous and nineteen or twenty and you have sat with prime ministers, kings and queens, the Pope? Do you go back home and take a job? What do you do to keep your sanity? You come back to the real world.'

    'Winning is great, sure, but if you are really going to do something in life, the secret is learning how to lose. Nobody goes undefeated all the time. If you can pick up after a crushing defeat, and go on to win again, you are going to be a champion someday.'

    'No matter what accomplishments you make, somebody helps you.'

    Imagine Wilma had just received a letter from a child saying 'One day I want to be a famous athlete like you.' What do these quotes reveal about Wilma's attitude to becoming a world-famous athlete? What thoughts would she put into her reply? Write the letter.

3. Wilma went on to do many other things. Find out the rest of her story at:

    www.lkwdpl.org/wihohio/rudo-wil.htm and
    gardenofpraise.com/ibdwilma.htm

    Afterwards, list what you think were her three greatest achievements after winning her gold medals.

Excellence

1972

Shane Gould

Excellence

Shane Gould

Swimmer, 100m, 200m, 400m, 800m (Munich 1972)

'For Shane, winning races, achieving gold medals and setting
world records were all incidental to the experience of swimming.'

Dennis Philips,
Australian Women at the Olympic Games

It was the 100m freestyle swimming final, and Shane was waiting.
This was always the strangest moment, the waiting, the time for
concentrating, just before the race.

She'd been training hard for this, had already broken five world
records—and was still only 15 years old. When the Australian team had
arrived for the Munich Games, she'd spoken to a reporter in German
and created a storm of interest. Who was this 'Australian Goldfish'?
So many people were waiting, wanting to see Shane win yet another
medal to match the gold she'd won a few days ago.

It was time. Someone was calling her name. 'Shane Gould. Australia!'
The crowd cheered, and Shane waved, forcing a smile despite the
distraction. She was the one everybody else had to beat, the golden
teenager racing with the adults. Two lengths, freestyle, against the
fastest swimmers in the world. She breathed deeply. Wiggle those
arms. Loosen up. Stay calm. Be ready for the starter pistol. Go.

She dived, bursting down into the water, surfacing, trying to storm
ahead, but something was different, wrong. She felt flat, lethargic, but
kept going. The energy wasn't there. Ignoring the other swimmers,
she put everything she knew into practice. Pushing through, gliding,
breathing, powering ahead to the other side. Tumble turn. Under,
round, pushing off again. Water flowing past, that lovely cool feeling.

Breathing. Pushing harder. Touch the side... and stop. It all happened so quickly, in just a few seconds.

She surfaced, cleared her eyes, and heard the crowd cheering. But it wasn't for her. Someone else had come first, and second. Shane was third. Third? Everyone had expected her to come first. And she was third. What are you meant to feel? Disappointed? Perhaps. She reached over the dividing lines, shaking hands with the winners, as you're meant to do. But this was something different, something new.

What happens when you don't win? Strangely, it didn't feel awful. Something inside her was saying, 'You don't have to win everything. You don't have to win. You just have to be here, doing what you do, doing it as best as you can, and enjoying it.' Resignation. Acceptance. It was a hard lesson to learn so quickly in front of the whole world, but, in a strange way, it felt good, grown-up even. She might be only 15, but something inside felt a little more adult. Even as Shane stood on the podium receiving her bronze medal, she was pondering this big idea—that winning wasn't everything.

However, there was a surprise waiting for her back at the Olympic village. She opened the door to her room to find it redecorated—with pink and white toilet tissue! 'Well done Shane!' squealed her room-mate, who ran over to give her a big hug. 'A bronze medal as well! Fantastic!' The hug helped a lot too.

Afterwards, there were more races for Shane, and more medals. The Olympics were soon over, and she came home with three gold medals, one silver and one bronze. Five medals in one Games—it was an incredible achievement. She loved her swimming, but what do you do when you've won just about everything? And what do you do when you lose? She had been training, driving herself hard to reach a peak of fitness and skill. She was satisfied that she had done the best she could on the days of her races. But what comes next? There was a lot to think about.

However, there was one important thing still to do. It was her mother's idea. One Sunday, Shane took her medals to church—and during a service, laid them on the table at the front. Five polished Olympic medals bearing her name, glittering against the clean white tablecloth. In her prayer, Shane said thank you to God for them, and that felt right.

There was more to her sport than winning. It was about trying hard, enjoying trying hard, respecting your competitors, asking for help, training, and overcoming disappointments too. There was a lot more to it than just winning awards and medals. Swimming was just a beautiful thing to be able to do. And it was a gift. Her talents came from somewhere else, someone else. And as Shane laid the medals down and stood back, it felt as if a great burden was lifting off her shoulders.

Activities

Lesson plan
Introduction

How do you concentrate? Is it possible to work too hard on getting something you really want?

Show this footage of Shane in action: **www.olympic.org/shane-gould**

Read aloud Shane's story. Afterwards emphasise the following key points:

- At 15, Shane was very young to be in an Olympic team and had to train very hard every day for years to be a world-beater.
- Because of her previous performance many people expected her to do well—and some criticised her for not winning every race.
- She won a race she didn't expect to win (200m) and came third in a race she expected to win (100m). Overall, she won five Olympic medals in 1972.
- After the Munich Games, Shane found being a sporting 'celebrity' very difficult, turned her back on it, and retired from competitive swimming at the age of 16.

Pupil activities

Religious Education

1. On returning home, Shane decided to thank God for her success in the Munich Games. As part of a church service, she placed her medals on the altar and said a prayer. Afterwards, she said, 'It had a profound and comforting effect on me. I could now see my achievements as something outside of myself, as a gift to be appreciated and a responsibility to be honoured, not as an ability to be owned and controlled.'

    How can a prayer have that sort of effect? What sorts of things might be in it? Some prayers include:

    Adoration—words of praise to God
    Confession—words expressing hopes, fears and regrets
    Thanks—words expressing gratitude
    Requests—words asking for help with something

    Write and illustrate the prayer that you think Shane might have said on that day.

2. A few years after the Games, Shane said, 'I was tired of trying to save myself from confusion, loneliness, self-deception and my disappointment in what I saw were the empty promises of fame.' Then she became interested in knowing more about Jesus. One of Shane's favourite Bible passages was: 'For it is by God's grace you have been saved, through faith. It is not the result of your own efforts, but God's gift, so that none can boast about it' (Ephesians 2:8–9).

    For Christians, 'grace' is God's free gift of love. In the middle of a page, draw a cartoon of someone drowning in the water. Around them, write or draw the things that Shane was feeling. Nearby, draw someone throwing a lifebelt inscribed with the word 'Grace'. Nearby, write or draw the things that might have attracted Shane towards Jesus and becoming a Christian.

PSE, Citizenship, Literacy

1. Many years later, Shane wrote: 'After the 100 metres race, I returned to my room where Bev had strung up pink and white toilet paper. She squealed with delight at my surprised reaction, then hugged and congratulated me. This was the best congratulations I've ever received from another athlete.' Why do you think Bev's greeting had such an impact on Shane? Make some links for a home-made paper-chain that say 'Well Done' to someone who could do with a pat on the back—then make the chain, and give it to them!

2. Shane was criticised by some Australians for 'only' getting a bronze medal for the 100m freestyle. 'Shane Fails' was one headline. Do you think that was fair? Why? In the changing room, some older American swimmers wore T-shirts saying 'All that Glitters is not Gould'. How do you think Shane felt under all that pressure? Create a diary entry that Shane might have written for the day of the 100m freestyle final, showing her feelings in the morning… and that evening, after the final. Think of an interesting title that could sum up her feelings at the beginning and the end of the day.

3. During the 1972 Games, there was a terrorist attack on the Olympic village after Shane's races, and some Israeli athletes were killed. This shocked everyone, and some people said the Games should stop. However, the organisers decided to complete the Games so other athletes could still compete in the events they had trained for. Do you think that was the right decision—or not? Research the event, list the reasons for and against continuing with the Games in 1972—and then give your own verdict.

4. 'If you make it into an Olympic team, you're good; if you make it into an Olympic final, you're great; and if you win an Olympic medal, you're a freak!'—Raelene Boyle, 200m silver medallist at Munich 1972.

    After the Games, Shane found it very hard to live with her successes, although she still loved to swim. What does this tell you about becoming a celebrity? Write a one-minute spoof advert/script for Celebrity, listing all the ways it can change your life—for the worse!

Friendship

1936

Jesse Owens

1936

Carl 'Luz' Long

Friendship

Carl Ludwig 'Luz' Long and Jesse Owens

Long jump, 100m, 200m (Berlin 1936)

'Friendships born on the field of athletic strife are the real gold of competition. Awards become corroded, friends gather no dust.'

Jesse Owens

Something wasn't right, but what? Jesse had made three jumps to qualify for the long jump finals, and none of them was good enough. The local favourite, Luz Long, was in the final, no question—he was on good form today. But Jesse wasn't, and he knew it. After all this training and getting a place in the United States Olympic team, he wasn't jumping well enough. And he only had one jump left. If it wasn't good, he would be out of the finals. This was Berlin in 1936—'Hitler's' Summer Games. And Adolf Hitler, Chancellor of Germany, had said that this was the time to show how white Aryan Germans could out-perform anyone with a darker skin—such as Jesse, who was African American. But now, with one more chance to qualify for the final, Jesse didn't know what to do. He was about to be called for his last jump, but there was nothing left to give. He was going to fail, and dreaded the thought.

He heard his name again, spoken in a German accent, and a warm hand on his shoulder. Was it the official in charge? He looked up. No. It was the German, his enemy, the man he had to beat. But the German was saying something.

'I'm Luz Long. I think I know what's wrong. You're like me. You're giving everything when you jump. But you're afraid of fouling again, aren't you?' Jesse nodded. 'So you're jumping short,' continued Luz.

'I was doing that last year in the Cologne Games. You just need to take-off from further back. That way, you can give everything. Come on. I'll put my towel down to mark the place for you.'

The take-off. Yes, it was so simple, but it needed Jesse's toughest opponent to point it out. What was happening? No matter. Luz marked a jumping-off place six inches forward from the jumping board, and stood back to watch as Jesse made his run. He started slowly with a slow stride, then ran faster, faster, then the take-off... and Jesse felt like he was flying. He landed. The officials got out their measuring tapes. Over 26 feet! Yes! He was in the finals! But why had it happened like this?

That evening, he met Luz for coffee, and asked him what he thought of Hitler's ideas, the ones about some races of people being better than others. Luz said they were all rubbish. *He* wasn't a Nazi, although he did love his country—and if there was a war, he'd serve in the army to defend Germany and his family. But Jesse knew this was a man who could be a good friend. So over the next few days, they kept meeting to drink coffee and swap stories as Jesse won more gold medals for the 100m, the 200m and relay.

Then came the day for the long jump final. Towards the end, as the other competitors dropped out, it became clear that the gold would go either to Luz or to Jesse. Luz took his final jump, an amazing effort. He flew through the air, landed—and set a new Olympic record. The German crowd in the stadium cheered their hero. But now it was Jesse's last turn. He ran, he leapt, he flew, landed—even further! But as he stumbled to his feet, Luz reached him first. 'I knew you did it!' the German whispered. And as the officials measured the jump and confirmed an even newer world record, Luz took Jesse by the arm and led him towards the German crowd, lifting Jesse's arm in the air as a champion. 'Jesse Owens! Jesse Owens!' Luz shouted, as loudly as he could. Some of the crowd joined in. 'Jesse Owens! Jesse Owens!' Others took up the cry. Soon, 100,000 Germans in Hitler's Olympic stadium were cheering the new champion. 'Jesse Owens! Jesse Owens! Jesse Owens! Jesse Owens!'

Activities

Lesson plan
Introduction

Ask if you can ever be friends with someone against whom you are competing.

Read aloud Luz and Jesse's story. Afterwards emphasise the following key points:

- In 1936, Hitler's Germany was a very difficult place to be if you weren't white. The Nazis believed some ethnic and racial groups were superior to others—and that black people couldn't be as good as white people at anything. Hitler wanted these Games to prove it.
- Other Western countries were not free from prejudice. As Jesse Owens said afterwards, 'Although I wasn't invited to shake hands with Hitler, I wasn't invited to the White House to shake hands with the (American) President either.'
- Luz was taking a real risk when he chose to be Jesse's friend. Hitler had refused to meet Jesse, the winner of four Olympic gold medals.
- Luz later died serving his country as a soldier during the Second World War.

Pupil activities

Religious Education

1. Find the photograph of US gold medallist Jesse Owens talking to German silver medallist Luz Long at the 1936 Olympic Games in Berlin at **berlin.iaaf.org**. Jesse and Luz were 'enemies' who chose to be friends. In the Sermon on the Mount (Luke 6:35), Jesus said 'Love your enemies and be good to them. Lend without expecting to be paid back. Then you will get a great reward, and you will be the true children of God in heaven.' Where it says 'without expecting to be paid back', some Bible

versions have it as 'without giving up on anyone'. What could this be saying about people who seem to be our enemies?

Create an illustrated poem or short story called 'The Children of Heaven' that explains your own thoughts and feelings about enemies and friends—and how people can change from one into the other.

2. Luz was an unexpected friend. When Jesus was asked 'Who is my neighbour?' he answered by telling the story of the Good Samaritan, but used a popular 'enemy' to demonstrate what compassion was really all about. Read the original Bible story (Luke 10:30–37), then tell your own modern version in a familiar setting—but using characters we would now think of as being enemies of each other. If you want to be really clever, retell it in the form of a rap/ manga strip-cartoon/ puppet play/ PowerPoint presentation with music and sound effects... or use some other media!

PSE, Citizenship, Literacy

1. 'It took a lot of courage for him to befriend me in front of Hitler... You can melt down all the medals and cups I have and they wouldn't be a plating on the twenty-four carat friendship that I felt for Luz Long at that moment'—Jesse Owens, after being advised and congratulated by Luz Long at the 1936 Olympics.

What does friendship mean? With a partner, produce the copy for a newspaper 'Wanted' advert for a good friend, exactly 20 words long, beginning like this: 'Wanted, a good friend—must be...'

2. Jesse didn't have to trust Luz's advice in the qualifying round—but he did, and it was a good choice. However, not all 'friends' are good for us. On the internet there are social networking websites for 'friends' to share their news, likes, dislikes, and much more—but it is all done online. What do you think could

be the dangers of 'making friends' like this? Research 'online safety' at **www.kidsmart.org.uk/**, listing what you think are the best three bits of advice offered—and why.

3. Luz and Jesse kept in touch afterwards by writing letters. In his last letter, written as a soldier shortly before he died in battle, Luz asked Jesse to 'Someday find my son... tell him about how things can be between men on this Earth.' What do you think he meant? What had their friendship proved? Imagine you are Jesse Owens and many years later you discover the address of Luz's adult son, Karl. What would you want to tell him about the events of 1936? Write the letter.

Courage

1908

Dorando Pietri

Courage

Dorando Pietri

Marathon runner (London 1908)

'Vincerò o morirò—I will win or I will die.'

Dorando Pietri

orando Pietri had started the marathon from behind, but he was determined to win. For years, he had been training for this moment at the London Games, and nothing was going to get in the way of his gold medal. But the race had started too quickly. Marathon runners have to pace themselves when they run 26 miles, but nobody seemed to be remembering that today. Too fast, too early and you're lost. But he had to keep up with them, even if it wasn't how he'd planned it. And the weather forecast had said it would be very warm, even for July—a bad sign if you're running.

Slowly, mile by mile, he worked his way through to the front. As they passed Wembley stadium, some of the front-runners were reduced to walking—with 9 miles to go. Dorando kept pushing, kept overtaking, choosing his moments to add a little speed *here*.... and *there*... but he was getting too tired too fast. He was now the front-runner by a long distance. Three miles to go—but his body was close to collapse.

Spectators were lining the route, cheering him on, but he could hardly hear them. His legs were aching, his lungs were wheezing. The stadium was in sight, the final mile. But everything was hurting. 'Vincerò o morirò.' 'I will win or I will die.' He kept repeating it. His mother knew him well. 'Please, Dorando, if things are going badly, drop out!' she'd warned. 'Please take care of yourself.' But the end was so close. 'Vincerò o morirò. Vincerò o morirò.' Step by step, he struggled on.

A wall of sound hit him as he entered the packed stadium and the crowd started cheering loudly as he came into sight. But Dorando wasn't running anymore. He was staggering, wandering like a man who was drunk. He'd collapsed in the entrance tunnel leading into the stadium, but rose to his feet again as a doctor appeared, and carried on running. Now he was on the track. 'Wrong way! Wrong way!' everybody shouted. What? Everything went black. He was on the ground. Someone was yelling 'Get a stretcher! Now!' Dorando seemed to wake up, and crawled to his feet again. 'For God's sake stop him!' somebody else shouted. 'He'll die. He's dying!' But Dorando's lips were still moving. 'Vincerò o morirò, vincerò o morirò.' I will win or I will die. He was back on his feet, half-walking, half-falling. As he wandered off the track, policemen and race officials kept steering him back towards the finish line. Meanwhile, one of the American runners had just entered the stadium and was catching up fast, but hardly anyone cared. All eyes were on Dorando.

Nearly there. Nearly there. A few more steps. 'Vincerò o morirò, vincerò o morirò.' Over the line. Finished. Victory. He collapsed, the stretcher arrived, and he was taken away to loud cheers. An official declared the result. 'First, and winner of the Greek Cup, Dorando Pietri... of Italy! Second... J.J. Hayes of the United States.' But was that true? The judges weren't so sure. Dorando had fallen at least four times on the last lap, and people had lifted, pushed him back on to his feet. Was he really the winner? After an hour, the judges changed the result, saying that the American had won instead. Dorando was disqualified for receiving assistance. What? The crowd were furious. It didn't seem fair. It was wrong! But the result stood. And then there were rumours flying about the stadium about the London crowd's hero, their 'little Italian pastrycook'. He was sick. He'd suffered a heart attack. Was he dead?

No. None of it was true. But in a few days there was news of a different sort. Queen Alexandra, who'd been in the stadium watching that final lap, wanted to meet Dorando—and present him with a special award, an engraved silver cup to mark his incredible determination in the race. Dorando hadn't won the marathon for 1908. But he had won something else, possibly something much more important... what was it?

See the moment...

www.youtube.com/watch?v=PZqPGpVxPKQ

A rather fetching video mixing original photographs and film of Dorando and *that* race.

www.youtube.com/watch?v=vTmcylObGJQ

A biographical video showing original footage of the final lap. Commentary is in Italian.

Activities

Lesson plan
Introduction

Ask what it means to be 'courageous'.

Read aloud the story, and show a video clip of the final 'lap' in the stadium. Afterwards emphasise the following key points:

- Dorando had been training hard for this race, after winning other prizes for his running. He knew he had it in him to win.
- Despite being first over the finishing line, he was disqualified because of assistance received. A successful marathon runner must win without receiving outside help.
- His desire to win endeared him to the British spectators. The idea for awarding him a special cup actually came from Sir Arthur Conan Doyle, the famous author who created Sherlock Holmes, who was there at the finish.
- Despite 'losing', Dorando's story made him more famous than many other runners who have come first!

Pupil activities

Religious Education

1. In the Bible, Jesus said that his kingdom would have a lot of surprises for his followers, adding these famous words, 'The first shall be last, and the last shall be first.' After losing his

gold medal, what do you think Dorando might have been feeling? Draw a silver cup in the middle of a page. On the left, list his possible feelings under the heading 'No Gold Medal'. Then on the right, under 'Special Award', list the new feelings or thoughts he might have had when he was given the special cup. Underneath, write Jesus' words.

2. Where did Dorando's courage come from? Athletes often talk about needing a Positive Mental Attitude (PMA) that encourages them to train hard and keep their 'eyes on the prize'. Saint Paul spoke of life being like an Olympic race in 1 Corinthians 9:24–26:

'Do you not know that in a race all the runners run, but only one gets the prize? Run in such a way as to get the prize. Everyone who competes in the games goes into strict training. They do it to get a crown that will not last, but we do it to get a crown that will last forever. Therefore I do not run like someone running aimlessly; I do not fight like a boxer beating the air.'

Paul's PMA was based on a life goal of following Jesus Christ. This faith and belief gave him a direction, an inner certainty and a courage that powered him up to change the whole world. So where could your own PMA come from? (Who do you really trust to encourage you—and what do they say?)

Create a diagram (like a race track) to show some personal targets for you to reach by the end of this academic year, or the ages of 11, 15, 18 or 30. Write them along the track. Next to the track draw some flags and banners with encouraging messages that could help you reach those goals. Then draw yourself at the beginning of the track, ready to run.

PSE, Citizenship, Literacy

1. Dorando didn't let his fear of dying stop him from doing his best. 'Courage' doesn't mean 'not being scared'! It means 'not allowing the fear to control us'. Sometimes fear can stop us from being brave—but talking about it and drawing it can help us to handle the fear. What frightens you? For fun, create a monster that's a detailed picture of some of the things that frighten you, and give it a funny name! (To protect sensitive feelings, teachers will need to decide whether these 'creatures' will be on display afterwards—and tell the pupils before they start.)

2. When we offer 'encouragement' to someone, we are actually trying to make them brave—to give them courage! What are the most encouraging words you have ever heard? Create a story in which somebody is really struggling with something they find very difficult and is close to giving up—until a friend or stranger offers them encouragement. Think hard about describing what the 'problem' is, and how it is finally resolved. Try to be realistic—do your best to explain the feelings that accompany 'not being able to do something', and how encouragement makes such a difference.

Determination

1996, 2000

Haile Gebrselassie

Determination

Haile Gebrselassie

Long-distance runner, 10,000m (Atlanta 1996, Sydney 2000)

'I'm not motivated by possessions or money. I just love running. I do lots of things, but nothing compares to running.'

Haile Gebrselassie

The starting pistol was raised. Bang! The runners leapt forward, jockeying for position as they took the first curve, some thrusting forward, others holding back, calculating the energy needed to push ahead, hold a lead or keep it all in reserve for later. Quick decisions. Instant choices. Legs, muscles, lungs, bodies pounding around the track.

Haile held himself back. Ten thousand metres, 25 laps, was plenty of time for opponents to get tired. And he was used to running for miles at a time. So, as they settled into the first few laps, his mind wandered. I'm actually here in Atlanta at last, he thought. Running in the Olympics for my country. My family.

He remembered running barefoot on the way to school, ten miles daily, holding, cradling, his precious schoolbooks that offered so much hope for the poor farmer's son. Even now, he still bent his left arm like that when he ran.

And then there was that first school race, when he left everyone behind. The young boy entering the 1500m against lots of older boys—streaking ahead and beating them all with 100m to spare! The watching crowd were ecstatic, rushing on to the track, carrying him on their shoulders, shouting 'Haile! Haile!'

Running. He just loved it. The thrill of being alive, the mind and body and spirit working together at speed.

Round another curve. He saw a TV reporter talking to camera, and remembered listening on his father's radio to live reports of the 1980 Moscow Games—when another Ethiopian won the 10,000m. And now it's my turn to try, he thought. My turn to show the world what we can do.

His father had wanted him to stay at home and help with the farm. He remembered the arguments. 'What can running get you? I need you here!' But the old man had finally agreed to it, bless him. He'll be watching me now on the village's only television, Haile thought. As I run for Ethiopia.

A few more laps. Haile slowly worked his way forward through the pack of other runners. He remembered moving to Addis, the nation's capital, and running along the tracks and foothills that surrounded the city, and being spotted by a running coach. 'You need a team,' said the coach. 'Do you really want to run? Then join our training programme.' All those exercise routines. All that discipline. All those hours spent on the move, improving your endurance, the will to win that lasts for miles and miles.

More laps. Half-way. He'd been a good runner, and was selected for international competitions. Antwerp. Stuttgart. Budapest. Gothenburg. Victories—was that what it was all about? Getting medals? But he also remembered walking into church, kneeling, and offering his running skills to God. If I win in Atlanta, he'd thought, I'll bring back my medal and leave it here in the church, as a sign. Not as a bargain. Not to buy God's approval. He'd worked hard, but without God all his efforts would be useless.

Not long now to the finish. Haile was second in the pack. He'd passed the others—but there was still the Kenyan runner out in front. A bell rang somewhere, signalling one final lap to go. Now it was time! Haile powered forward, overtaking the Kenyan, pushing ahead. But could he keep the pace?

He was in front, but for how long? Haile glanced back. No! Keep looking ahead! Nearly there! Keep going! The finishing line's ahead! Crowds are cheering! He was nearly there, don't slow down.

Over the line at last. I've finally done it, he thought. For my family, for my people, for my God. I've won.

He bent over to catch his breath, felt people patting him on the back, shaking his hand. Someone gave him a flag to hold, the flag of Ethiopia, his homeland. Haile jogged to the grass verge, took off his running shoes, and did one more circuit of the stadium, waving to the crowd, proudly carrying his nation's flag and wearing a wide smile. And at the medal award ceremony, when they played the Ethiopian national anthem to celebrate Haile's win, he was weeping—with joy.

Activities

Lesson plan
Introduction

After checking for hazards on the floor, ask your pupils to remove their shoes (and socks? You decide...), walk around the room and then return to replace their footwear. Discuss in pairs what it felt like, and list the places where you might normally go barefoot. Share some comments, pointing out that in some parts of the world it is normal for children their age to travel barefoot everywhere because shoes are too expensive.

Read aloud Haile's story and, if possible, show some recorded video footage of this race (10,000m, Atlanta 1996) which can be found in various places on the internet. (The final section of Leslie Woodhead's 1999 film *Endurance* usefully replays elements of Haile's life story, intercut with race footage.)

Afterwards emphasise the following key points:

- Haile was born and raised in a single-roomed hut on a farm in a very poor part of the world. As he grew up, Ethiopia experienced drought, famine and civil war.
- This background (and the high altitude) helped to make Haile strong and tough—he was used to making long journeys on foot to fetch water or get to school.

- Running is now a high-profile popular sport in Ethiopia and it carries a lot of national pride—especially when Ethiopians race Kenyans!
- Haile's successes in running later won him a lot of prize money, which he used to build up several successful businesses, employ hundreds of local people, and fund the building of schools and hospitals.

Pupil activities

Religious Education

1. As an Orthodox Christian, Haile had strong positive beliefs that affected his sporting performance. He said:

   'I have to work hard, but without God, all my efforts are useless.'

   'When you believe in something, you believe in yourself as well. I believe in God.'

   'I go to a church and pray, not just to pray to God, but at the same time to pray for myself. Your body is always ready to do what you ask it. That's why believing is very important. I am a religious person. My family taught me how to pray.'

   Write a prayer that you think Haile might have prayed in church before going to compete in the Atlanta Games. Then write the prayer you think he might have said when he returned, carrying his gold medal. Illustrate this with a picture of an Ethiopian cross, examples of which can be found on Google images.

2. The Ethiopian Cross is an important symbol in the Orthodox Church and highly symmetrical in design. You can make the basic shape by folding a square piece of paper in four and then cutting it similarly to the way in which we make 'snowflake' designs. It can be decorated with silver paper

and other materials to achieve a 'jewelled' effect. For more background and lesson material relating to this and other world cross motifs, see Martyn Payne and Betty Pedley's extremely useful book A-cross the World, which is available from Barnabas as a download at: **www.barnabasinschools. org.uk/**.

PSE, Citizenship, Literacy

1. Find a picture of the Ethiopian flag. Why do you think Haile was waving it and carrying it so proudly after his race? Draw and label the flag (or make it out of coloured sticky paper) and add in thought bubbles around its edge what you think Haile's thoughts would have been, both at that moment after the race, and during the medal ceremony.

2. Ethiopia is what's called a 'developing nation', with most people there having a lower standard of living than experienced in the West. But Haile still gets cross at the way some people judge his country unfairly. 'The thing that really offends me,' he says, 'is that the most important value in the 21st century is how much money you have. They say the most important thing in the world is to be rich. But money is not everything!' Read his story again, listing under the flag (from activity 1) what he might think the most important things really are. Tick the ones you especially agree with.

3. 'Determination' can mean many things. Which parts of Haile's story teach you the most important things about it? Create an illustrated haiku or tanka poem entitled 'Determination' that sums up these thoughts and feelings.

4. Some Ethiopians would like Haile to go into politics when he stops running. He says: 'If I were prime minister, I would send everyone to school. Education is all. That is what I would love to do for this country: educate it.'

Send My Friend To School is a charity (supported by many UK schools) that campaigns to allow more children around the world to have an education. Visit their website to find out more, then design a bookmark or lapel badge with words and symbols that sum up their key message. Consider planning a charity event to raise money for this cause. See: **www.sendmyfriend.org/**.

5. Haile's advice for anyone thinking of getting into sport:

'You need three things to win: discipline, hard work and, before everything maybe, commitment. No one will make it without those three. Sport teaches you that.'

'It is not enough just to win the race, it is how you handle the lessons, how you improve. Some athletes, after they have won something, because they are not disciplined, they don't make the most of it.'

'I am not hungry for success, I am hungry for running. I am disciplined. Sometimes when I meet people and they say, "What do I have to do to be like you?" I say, "Look, sport has to come from inside." You can't look at someone and say, "I want to be like you." The desire has to be yours.'

Where do you think he learned this? Try to sum up his key ideas in as few words as possible. What pictures or symbols would convey these thoughts? Use them to create a T-shirt design that includes at least one positive image connected to Ethiopia.

Inspiration

1924

Eric Liddell

Inspiration

Eric Liddell

Runner, 200m, 400m (Paris 1924)

'I just don't like to be beaten.'

Eric Liddell

The British team were baffled when they heard about it. What was wrong? Why couldn't their best sprinter run his race? 'It's for the Olympics!' they said. 'You're one of the fastest men in the world!'

Eric Liddell wouldn't have it. 'Because that race is on the Lord's Day. It's the Sabbath. I'm not running on a Sunday.'

The Paris Olympics were a few months away, and the race details had just been released. Eric's best event was the 100m sprint—but the qualifying finals for the 100m, the 4x100m relay and the 4x400m relays would all take place on a Sunday—the Christian Sabbath. And Eric never ran on the Sabbath. Even though 100m was his best distance by far.

'So what are you going to do?' asked his team-mates.

'Train for the 400m—I've done well in it before.'

'But it's not your best event.'

But Eric wouldn't be moved. By the time of the Paris Olympics, he was as ready as he'd ever be. But would his beliefs cost him the gold medal? Many saw him as the sprinter who'd lost his chance to win the 100m for his country. Had he done the right thing? Yes—but some newspapers had even called him a traitor, and that hurt.

It was Friday morning, the day of the 400m final. He'd trained hard for it and qualified well, but already the summer weather was stifling. Some were calling this stadium 'the furnace' because of the

55

baking heat. The runners lined up, each of them crouching down with a trowel to shape their own particular starting line, digging out a small pit for each foot to give maximum thrust when they heard the starting pistol.

Eric was thinking hard. He wanted to win. But he'd sacrificed the 100m. Was it possible to do it in a different event? The speed was different, the timing was different. All that training, all that sacrifice. At the stadium, he'd opened a note given him at his hotel—and read these words:

'In the old book it says "He that honours me, I will honour."
Wishing you the best of success always.'

An encouragement from the British team physio. Eric smiled at the memory, then turned back to his preparations. From somewhere in the stadium, he could hear bagpipes, the sound of Scotland, his home. Now he was ready. The trowels were collected, and he followed his normal custom of walking along the starting line, shaking hands with his opponents—then returned to his lane and crouched down, staring ahead. There were just two straights and a curve on this track. He was on the outside lane, and would have to get to the curve first.

The starter gave his final instructions. Get set. The runners silently tensed up, straining to hear the sound. Crack! went the pistol. Up, out, running as fast as possible, pushing forward. Eric was streaking ahead, like a sprinter. It was the only thing he knew. Striding out, knees pumping. Pushing, pushing along the straight towards the first curve, leaving the others behind. He was round the curve, but would he run out of steam? You can't sprint 400m. No one can. But he kept running. The others were catching up, gaining on him, getting closer. It was the final straight.

'Those who honour me, I will honour.' Eric put everything into the last 100m, the power was coming from somewhere. Head back, chin forward, mouth open, knees jumping, arms waving in the air. Pushing forward again... pushing... and over the line. Finished.

First. He'd won. 400m. 47.6 seconds. A new Olympic record. Unbelievable!

Eric collected his gold medal, but didn't stay in the stadium for long, and went back to his hotel to clean up. That Sunday, he was going to be preaching in a Paris church, and he needed time to prepare his words, and think. The newspapers that had said so many horrible things about him were now calling him a marvel. But what they said didn't matter now. He had other things to do that were much more important.

Activities

Lesson plan
Introduction

Are there some things that are so special to you, so precious, you'll hold to them no matter what? Explain that many people have a personal core belief that gives them a strength and sense of direction for their life. But what happens if that core belief comes up against something that refuses to recognise it? What do you sacrifice? Many people have had to give up all sorts of good things to follow their beliefs.

Read aloud Eric's story. You might wish to show a clip from the Oscar-winning 1981 film *Chariots of Fire* as part of this—especially the footage of Eric's race.

Afterwards emphasise the following key points:

- As a Christian, Eric had refused to compete in his best events (100m sprint and relay) because it would mean running the qualifying heats on a Sunday, something that went against his core beliefs.
- Instead, he trained for the 200m and 400m, which needed a different training and strategy, although he still ran them like a 100m sprint.
- He won a bronze medal for the 200m, and gold for his famous 400m run.

- He was born in China to Scottish parents who were Christian missionaries, and after the Olympics was soon training to be a missionary himself. He spent most of his adult life in China, looking after people and teaching them about Jesus—and died there.

Pupil activities

Religious Education

1. Sometimes our personal beliefs can clash with those of others. Muslim athletes from many nations may have problems competing in the Games during Ramadan because during that time a devout Muslim doesn't take in food or water during the daylight hours—which causes problems for athletes hoping to achieve a personal best in the summer Games, when the days are longer. Eric faced a similar problem about running on the Christian Sabbath. What feelings experienced by Eric (in 1924) would be similar to those of modern Muslim athletes?

   Draw two faces on a page, labelled 'Eric Liddell—1924' and 'Muslim athlete today'. Write some thought bubbles for both of them in the run-up to the Games, with sentences inside beginning, 'I wish...', 'I believe...' and 'I hope...' Would any of their thoughts be similar? Why?

2. In 1991, a memorial headstone was unveiled at the former prison camp in China where Eric died. Apart from his personal details, it includes words taken from the biblical book of Isaiah (40:31): 'They shall mount up with wings as eagles; they shall run and not be weary.' What do you think this is saying about the life of Eric Liddell as a runner and as a Christian? Looking ahead, what words would you choose to have inscribed on your own headstone that sum up the way you'd like your life to be? Design what you think Eric's memorial would look like. Then, if you have time, design your own.

3. Eric didn't want to run on the Christian Sabbath (Sunday) because he firmly believed in it being a special day dedicated to God. Nowadays, Sunday in this country is treated by many as just another day for work, shopping or leisure. What do you think about that? Should there be a special day that's different from the others? Keep Sunday Special is a campaign group who argue that Sundays need to be much less busy. With a partner, research their reasons at **www.keepsundayspecial.org.uk/Web/** and sum up their main arguments in 50 words or less. What would their opponents argue, against this? Use these thoughts to create a summary of the debate, and in conclusion give your own opinion about how Sundays should be used.

4. Many years later, in China, Eric was looking after some teenagers in a prison camp, and spent a lot of time giving them positive things to do in a very difficult place. He was still passionate about not playing games on a Sunday. However, some of the teenagers wanted to have a hockey match on a Sunday (boys against girls) and organised it themselves—but it turned into a fight because there was no referee. On the following Sunday, Eric came out to referee for them. Remember that he had refused to run on a Sunday for an Olympic gold medal. What does this extra story tell you about him? Why do you think he broke the rule he had kept for years? Two of his favourite Bible passages were 1 Corinthians 13:1–13 and Matthew 5:1–12. Read them, draw a hockey stick, and copy out some verses that you think would have meant a lot to Eric as he was wondering what to do about the teenagers.

PSE, Citizenship, Literacy

1. The design of Olympic medals changes for every city that holds the Games. Design the two faces of a gold medal that could be awarded to Eric after the Paris 1924 Olympics. On the back, write his name, his winning event—and a symbol or picture that sums up something special about his story,

especially his resistance to doing what others wanted because he thought it was wrong.

2. Before... and after. Imagine you are a very patriotic sportswriter reporting for the *Daily Mail* in 1924. You have just been told that Great Britain's best hope for a gold medal has refused to run for religious reasons. What would you think and say about Eric? Write two 'opinion pieces' for the newspaper for the day before the race (Thursday 10 July) and the evening after the race (Friday 11 July.) Your second piece might be rather different! (Eric's place in the 100m race was taken by Harold Abrahams—who eventually won—but you won't know that yet, will you?)

Equality

1988–2000

Lilo Ljubisic

Equality

Lilo Ljubisic

*Discus and shot put (Seoul 1988, Barcelona 1992,
Atlanta 1996, Sydney 2000)*

'There are many things in your life that will catch your eye but
only a few will catch your heart. Pursue those.'

Lilo Ljubisic

Lilo couldn't believe what Mrs Henderson had just said.
'Volleyball?' asked Lilo. 'You actually want me to play volleyball?
But I can hardly see to hit the ball!'

'Don't rule yourself out because of that,' the PE teacher replied. 'I
think you could be a great server. You've got the height for it, and I
see you estimating distances all the time as you move around school.
I think you could have the muscle and skill to be rather good at
volleyball if you practise.'

It seemed a crazy idea. Lilo had suffered from poor eyesight for
years, ever since a doctor gave her the wrong treatment for a common
childhood illness. Now, normal light hurt her eyes. She had to walk
under a big black umbrella on bright days, wearing a baseball cap with
a wide brim, with large sunglasses to block out the glare. When reading
at school, she had to hold the books so close to her face that her nose
was often smudged from the ink. As for PE lessons, she normally sat
out, preferring study in the library to sitting on the sidelines, watching
other kids participate in activities she could only dream of playing.

But volleyball? Mrs Henderson was insistent. So, after being given
a crash course in serving, and after Mrs Henderson had worked out
a way to help her estimate the heights and distances of a volleyball
court, Lilo continued practising against the gym wall and in the

63

backyard of her home until she got the serve just right. She'd cradle the ball in her left hand, drawing back the right at waist height, punching the ball up and over to land just inside the opponent's side of the net. And practice makes perfect, even if you're visually impaired.

Two weeks later, Mrs Henderson organised a volleyball game for the PE class, saying that this time Lilo would be playing too, but only as a server for her team. (Usually, volleyball players switch positions throughout the game.) The two captains picked teams and Lilo was, naturally, picked last. But then it was her team's turn to begin. Lilo took her place as server on the court and was handed the ball. Ready? She held the ball, swung... and served. Thud! The sound of a ball hitting the ground...

'What happened? Where did it go?' asked Lilo.

Someone shouted, 'One nothing. An ace!' Lilo had gained a point! The ball had sailed over the net and hit the opponent's side of the court faster than anyone could touch it. Lilo served again, scoring another point. And another point. And another. Lilo sent fifteen straight serves sailing over the net to win the game for her team with hardly anybody else touching the ball—except to fetch it and bring it back to her.

And so a new life began for the teenager. Lilo's mother had always told her that God had a special plan for her life, and sport began opening doors. At university, Lilo took up goalball, a team sport designed for the blind, and was soon playing in competitions. By the age of 23, she was playing goalball for the Canadian Paralympic team. After that came an interest in field athletics. She decided to specialise in the throwing events, concentrating on shot put and discus. It was hard work, but she was determined her disability wouldn't get in the way of doing her best. A team coach provided guidance, training and fitness routines. Lilo rediscovered the Christian faith of her early years and was baptised. She also married. More doors were opening.

Over the next few years, Lilo won gold, silver and bronze medals at the Paralympics in Seoul, Barcelona, Atlanta and Sydney, and set new world records for throwing the shot put and discus. It wasn't easy, and there were lots of difficulties to face and more choices to make. But sport had shown her how to face challenges and sometimes overcome them too. It was all about having a belief in your own value and your ability to choose. And so much of this started all those years ago, with someone who had first chosen to believe in her.

Activities

Lesson plan
Introduction

Ask pupils to discuss in pairs what choices they had to make before arriving in school this morning. Then ask them to imagine how those choices might be affected if they were disabled in some way—such as being partially sighted, hearing impaired or having to use a wheelchair.

Read aloud Lilo's story. Afterwards emphasise the following key points:

- Lilo was born sighted, but a childhood illness and poor medical treatment led to many years of increasing blindness and pain.
- At school in both Yugoslavia and Canada, Lilo experienced a lot of teasing and bullying from other children because of the way her disability made her look different from others.
- As a young adult, Lilo discovered the power of choice. She didn't have to accept the limits that others placed on her because she was blind.
- Sport opened up a whole new set of possibilities for Lilo. She is now retired from athletics—but still campaigns for the rights of children facing difficulties like hers, and uses her story to encourage young people to make the most of the choices in front of them.

Pupil activities

Religious Education

1. Here is some advice from Lilo for young people.

'First, challenge yourself to do the best you can with the talents with which you are blessed. It is very important to set goals and dream big. Being able to visualise your dream brings you closer to your achievement—especially in my case since I'm blind. Second, grasp the power and strength in teamwork. No one stands alone. Find people who will support your dream and help you to make it a reality. Third, focus on what you can do, and not on what you can't.'

'Faith is the basis of my life, the sustaining power to overcome adversity. In the shadowy, cold valleys, we realise we aren't self-sustaining—and need to lean on God's love and mercy.'

'You can do it. With courage, commitment, and hard work, you can achieve your goals. You have the choice.'

In the Bible, someone wrote, 'Faith is being sure of what we hope for, and being certain of what we do not see' (Hebrews 11:1). Copy this quote out and draw Lilo's sunglasses. Lilo's Christian faith helps her to believe in herself and her abilities. It gives her an inner strength. Now draw yourself on a page. Around the picture, draw or list the things that make you strong—think especially about the things that help you to believe in yourself and your ability to handle challenges. (Who do you trust to help you?) If you wish, copy out a suitable quote from Lilo that you agree with, or a good piece of advice from somebody that gave you inner strength.

PSE, Citizenship, Literacy

1. Lilo said, 'We are the only beings on this planet that have the power of Choice.' List 20 choices you will have to make today that an animal (such as a dog or cat) can't make. Look at your

list again. Put a star next to the ones that might be important in a week's time. Circle the ones that could be important for you in a year's time. Underline the ones that might be important in five years' time. Discuss your list with a partner. Over the next year, what are the most important choices you might have to make, and why? Write about them.

2. Lilo says, 'Years ago, I would show up at local all-comers tournaments. The event organisers would tell me I wasn't welcome. That kind of rejection marked me; it served as the impetus for me to make change. I have bruises all over my body from hitting barriers. But once I broke through those, I could look back and see there was a hole. Now, 20 years later, there's no trace there was ever a wall there.'

Draw a figure of Lilo standing next to a large wall made up of large bricks. On the bricks, write some of the excuses people might have made when telling Lilo that she couldn't compete in an athletics competition for shot put or discus. Nearby, draw a bulldozer. By the bulldozer, write some of the answers that Lilo might have given.

3. Lilo was born in Yugoslavia—at that time, there was no special provision for partially sighted children apart from a special school a hundred miles away from her family home. Her parents campaigned to get her instead into a local school that would accept a child with special needs. In the end, the family emigrated to Canada to find a school that would give Lilo the support she needed. Using a map of your own school, think about how your school is designed, built and run. How has it been adapted to help people with special needs and disabilities? Start by thinking about wheelchair access for entrances, exits and doors, including ramps—but are there other things too? Could you spot something else that needs doing—and suggest (or even design) a solution for it? (Think of the entrance hall, the playground equipment...)

4. Research the events on offer nowadays in the Paralympics, and create a poster explaining and celebrating the most interesting events. The BBC sport website is a good source for researching the history of the Paralympics: **news.bbc.co.uk/ sport1/hi/other_sports/disability_sport/3628745.stm**.

Assemblies
and Collective Worship

Assembly 1

What can we learn from the Games?

<table>
<tr>
<td>Aim:</td>
<td>To re-enact moments from the Ancient Greek Games, and stress the importance of personal beliefs.</td>
</tr>
<tr>
<td>Props:</td>
<td>Six pre-arranged volunteers willing to make a spectacle of themselves, four of them wearing sports kit, the others clad creatively as a 'herald' and as a 'priest'. Four 'offerings' for the Temple of Zeus (plastic money), a collection plate and 'laurel wreaths' for the winners. A map of Ancient Greece showing some key locations.</td>
</tr>
<tr>
<td>Bible passage:</td>
<td>Hebrews 12:1b–2a.</td>
</tr>
</table>

Introduction: the Ancient Greek Games

Have you ever wondered how the Games came about? It all goes back into history. The first part of the Games is named 'The Olympics' after the Ancient Greek Games that were held alongside the massive Temple of Zeus (king of the gods) at the city of Olympia. Greece then was a group of city-states that were often at war with each other—and one story says that the Games were invented to calm things down. The games were held for one month, every four years, and during that time wars were cancelled so that the athletes could travel safely to and from Olympia. The modern Games were reinvented just over a hundred years ago—and take place in different cities around the whole world. But just how different are they?

71

Looking deeper: how they used to do things at Olympia

Bring out your volunteers. Give out labels/'standards'/signs for the different city-states—Athens, Sparta, Rhodes, Corfu—and place them at different corners of the hall. Appoint 'Milo' your herald and 'Solon' your match official/priest. Introduce them. The herald Milo is there to summon the athletes and announce the different events, and Solon is there to receive offerings and act as a starter and judge.

Solon:	Herald, announce the Games.
Milo:	I hereby pronounce that the Olympic Games will take place in two weeks' time at Olympia. All wars should stop, and all athletes should buy their travel tickets now! *(Milo goes around the hall collecting athletes from the different cities, who arrive back at Olympia.)*
Solon:	Bring your offerings to the god Zeus.*(He holds out his collection plate and receives the offerings.)* Will you compete fairly? And keep the rules, in the name of Zeus?
Athletes:	We will!
Solon:	Let the Games begin.

Only free men could take part—no women and no slaves. The sports included horse riding, chariot-racing, running races, boxing, wrestling and extreme wrestling, running while wearing armour, and the throwing of the javelin and the discus—and writing poetry! Let's see who's going to win this morning!

Safely stage three events in the hall for your competitors, with Solon as the final judge: these can be acted out or genuine, but always consider Health and Safety. For example:

- 'Throwing the javelin or discus' using plastic drinking straws and paper plates (up over the seated audience?).

72

- 'Standing long jump' (along a long PE jumping mat), a genuine Ancient Greek Olympic sport.
- 'Poetry'—how many words can you come up with that rhyme with the name... Bill? (Competitors have one minute to jot their own lists on whiteboards.)

Afterwards, have the winners presented with laurel crowns by Solon, and give all the competitors a round of applause as they return to their places.

Long ago, a mystery author in the Bible wrote that life was like an Olympic race—and Jesus was like a winning athlete and trainer.

> 'Therefore, since we are surrounded by such a great cloud of witnesses, let us throw off everything that hinders and the sin that so easily entangles. And let us run with perseverance the race marked out for us, fixing our eyes on Jesus, the pioneer and perfecter of our faith.'

Throw off everything that hinders? The Ancient Greek athletes usually competed completely naked, so nothing got in the way! But this mystery writer saw that true athletes train hard, listen to their trainer and don't let anything get in the way of doing their best. And he saw a connection—that people can allow all sorts of things to spoil their lives if they're not careful. But for Christians, Jesus could help them stay on track if they listened to him and trusted him because he'd already been through all this and won. Belief is a powerful part of being an athlete—and what you believe can affect everything else you do! How could your beliefs change the way you do things today?

Meditation

Think of a time when you've found life to be difficult. What helped you get through that time? Silently say thank you for it.

Prayer

Lord Jesus, thank you for offering to be a friend and helper, because you knew what it was like to suffer. When life gets tough, help me to listen to you. Amen.

Thought for the day

The Ancient Greek word for the Games was 'Agones', from which we get the word 'agony', which means 'extreme pain'. For them, being a successful athlete meant being ready to go through a lot of struggle, suffering and pain to gain a victory. Are you ready to face difficulties to reach your targets?

Assembly 2

How might the Games make the world a better place?

Aim: To consider how a simple idea can change things.

Props: Pictures of John Ian Wing as a teenager, and Olympic opening and closing ceremonies.

Bible passage: Galatians 3:28.

Introduction: when sport goes bad...

Have you ever played a game that went wrong—that ended with people feeling really angry with each other? When the Olympics were first reinvented by Pierre de Coubertin a hundred years ago, he hoped that it would increase 'friendly understanding among nations'. It hasn't always worked like that. Sometimes, there's been cheating, name-calling, arguments about who's really won, arguments about rules, and about who should be playing and who shouldn't... But there've been some good things too. This assembly is about one of them.

Looking deeper: John Ian Wing's letter

The 1956 Olympic Games took place in Melbourne, Australia. This wasn't an easy time for the world. Many people could still remember the pain and suffering of the Second World War, and there were other problems too. Some teams used the Games to 'get their own back' on their enemies. The water polo final between Russia and Hungary turned into an ugly fight because the Hungarians were furious at how their country had been invaded by the Russian army. Egypt, Iraq and Lebanon refused to compete because Egypt had been invaded by Britain, France and Israel. And the Chinese government were unhappy about Taiwan taking part.

But something else happened. A Chinese boy (living in Australia) had a very simple idea, and decided to share it. So, as the Games were progressing, John Ian Wing wrote a letter to Kent Hughes, one of the organisers. (See letter opposite.)

John didn't sign the letter, because he feared getting his parents into trouble. But Kent Hughes was so impressed, he took the letter and showed it to the other organisers—and they decided to rearrange the closing ceremony. The athletes wouldn't march in teams, waving their flags. Instead of marching as national teams, they would parade as one people. So that's what happened—and afterwards, everyone agreed it was a wonderful thing to do.

Of course, this hasn't stopped countries since then from fighting and going to war. But it gives a hint of how things could be.

In the Bible, Saint Paul wrote a famous letter that talked about how all the differences between people could melt away when Jesus came into the picture.

'You are all children of God through faith in Jesus Christ... There is neither Jew nor Greek, slave nor free, male nor female, for you are all one in Christ Jesus.'

Galatians 3:28

For Paul, God's love could drive out the need for any flags. People didn't have to be enemies just because they were different. They could all become children of the same loving Heavenly Father.

Some people think that John Ian Wing's letter saved the Games, by stopping it from becoming a battleground. His big idea has been used at every Olympic closing ceremony since then—the athletes still march together at the end, as one nation instead of many.

Meditation

'Writing a letter of complaint is easy, but if you really want to try and make a difference, offer a solution as well!'—John Ian Wing

Dear Friend

I am a Chinese boy and have just turned 17 years of age. Before the Game I thought everything would be in a muddle, however I am quite wrong, it is the most successful Game ever staged. One of the reasons for its Great success is the friendliness of Melbourne people. Overseas people would agree with me that Melbourne people are the most friendly people in the world.

Mr Hughes, I believe it has been suggested, that a march should be put on during the Closing Ceremony and you said it couldn't be done. I think it can be done. The march I have in mind is different than the one during the Opening Ceremony, and will make these games even greater, During the march there will only be 1 NATION. War, politics and nationality will be all forgotten. What more could anybody want, if the whole world could be made as one nation? Well you can do it in a small way.

This is how I think it can be done—no team is to keep together and there should be no more than two team mates together, they must be spread out evenly, and THEY MUST NOT MARCH, but walk freely and wave to the public, let them walk around twice on the track. When they stop, the public will give them three cheers.

I'm certain everybody (even yourself) would agree with me, that this would be a great occasion for everybody and no one would forget it. It will show the whole world how friendly Australia is.

Prayer

Father God, thank you for thoughtful people like John Ian Wing. Help us all to find ways to make friends with other people, especially those who are different from us, just as Jesus did. Amen.

Song: 'Make me a channel of your peace'

Thought for the day

How different would the Games be, if they took out all the national flags, anthems and uniforms? Would it be better? Why?

You can visit John's own website at **www.johnwing.co.uk/**. It contains other useful links.

Assembly 3

Why do we have the Paralympics?

Aim: To explore positive Paralympic values about disability.

Props: Netball/basketball net. A wheelchair (if you have one in school), a chair, a basketball/netball, three willing pupils who can 'shoot baskets' in basketball or netball.

Bible passage: Luke 14:16–24.

Introduction

How would you feel if you heard there was a party going on that you ought to be invited to, but nobody sent you an invitation?

How would you feel if you saw people playing a game but they didn't ask you to join in, because they thought you wouldn't be good enough?

That's how it sometimes feels to be disabled—if there's something wrong with your sight, your hearing, for example, or if you have to spend a lot of your life in a wheelchair. The problem sometimes isn't the things that your body can't do—it's about other people's attitudes. They think that the disability decides who you are, and think they know what you can or can't do. But disabled people can be full of surprises!

Looking deeper: the Paralympics

Ask three pupils to take turns at 'shooting a basket' from a standing position. Then ask them to repeat it from a sitting position in a chair/wheelchair. Afterwards, ask them how it changes the challenge.

In 1948, London was getting ready to host the Summer Olympics—when someone working in a hospital had an idea. Dr Ludwig Guttmann worked at Stoke Mandeville Hospital in Buckinghamshire, a place that helps people with spinal injuries. Many of these people were disabled ex-servicemen who had been injured fighting in the Second World War. Many doctors thought that there was nothing more that could be done for them. But Dr Ludwig didn't think so. He saw sport and games as an excellent way to help people regain their self-confidence after suffering terrible injuries—so why not have the hospital run its own sports competitions as part of the treatment? They tried wheelchair polo, basketball, archery... and it all worked. Competition was fun and exciting for these young men. Sport was giving them a new zest for life!

So Dr Ludwig arranged for Stoke Mandeville to host its own Olympics with other hospitals at the same time as the London Games—but with sports designed for wheelchair users. Four years later, they did it again, with a Dutch team joining in. Every four years, the idea grew. By 1960, the competition was called the Paralympics (or Parallel Olympics), and it was held in Rome with 400 athletes from 23 countries. By 1976, there was a Winter Paralympic competition too, and more events for people with other disabilities. It just keeps getting bigger and better.

So why is this important?

Jesus told a Bible story about a king holding a party and how it all went wrong—but then it went right. (See story opposite.)

So then—why do you think some of the guests didn't bother to come? (*Because they didn't think it was important enough.*)

Which people really appreciated the party? Why? (*They weren't used to being treated as valued guests.*)

The Paralympics are a little like that great feast. Sometimes, the Olympics can go wrong—when sporting superstars are treated like celebrities who are better than anyone else. But the Paralympics show what the Olympics ought to be—a celebration of what people *can* do, not what they *can't*. It's about valuing everyone, and giving everyone a chance to shine.

What's more, Paralympic athletes work hard at their sports just like Olympic athletes do—and whether they win a medal or not, they can teach us a lot about discovering and using our own talents to the best of our ability. Do you get hung up about what you *can't* do? How about spending more time thinking about discovering what you *can* do—and working on it?

The great feast

There was once a rich farmer who planned a big birthday party in his barn. There would be music, dancing and fantastic food. He invited all the local people who knew him, and they all naturally said 'yes' when they were given an invitation. But on the day of the party something weird happened. All the guests said 'no'. They were too busy doing other things on their own farms. That made the rich farmer really angry. All that time and effort spent planning a party... gone to waste!

Then he told his servants, 'Right! We're going to have a party anyway! Go out into the town, and invite anyone who wants to come, anyone who'd love to hear some decent music, have a dance or eat some decent food! Bring anyone who feels left out, especially anyone who's disabled, anyone whose eyes, ears and legs don't work very well, or anyone who doesn't fit in. It doesn't matter if they don't know me, because they're going to, now! Because we're going to party!'

So the servants did. All sorts of people came, and when they arrived at the barn, they were treated as honoured guests. All night there was live music, singing, dancing, and good food for everybody. It wasn't the party everyone expected. In fact, it was even better!

Meditation

Your body is an amazing gift—including the parts that you think don't work so well. When was the last time you were thankful for being able to use it? How about saying thank you, silently, now?

Prayer

Lord Jesus, in your story, you invited everyone to the great feast for the time of their lives. Help us all to enjoy each other's company, and enjoy each other's differences. Amen.

Thought for the day

Everybody is one accident away from becoming disabled.

Acknowledgments

With special thanks to Shane Gould, Lilo Ljubisic,
Haile Gebrselassie and Jos Hermans
for their help and advice.

Bibliography

Shane Gould, *Tumble Turns*, Harper Sports, 2000.

Lilo Ljubisic, *The Challenge of Change*, audio download, liloinspires.com, 2011.

Sally Magnusson, *The Flying Scotsman: A Biography*, Quartet Books, 1981.

Jesse Owens with Paul Neimark, *Jesse: The Man Who Outran Hitler*, Ballantine Books, 1978.

Story Assemblies for the School Year

36 assemblies with five-minute stories, teacher's notes and RE follow-up

Edward J. Carter

This book is full of memorable stories, designed to engage and delight pupils at primary level. The stories are essentially parables about God and the events in the Bible, creatively told to help children understand the big story of God's love for the world.

There are six themes in total, each with its own easy-to-make storytelling prop. The stories within each theme are divided into six weekly episodes, covering a wide range of contemporary values and topics. Together the stories cover the whole school year, with a key theme and a story in six parts for each half-term period.

As well as being ideal for collective worship, there are practical follow-up ideas to help children connect with the stories in the classroom. The six themes cover:

- God's creation
- The message of the Old Testament prophets
- Stories about Christian values
- The story of Holy Week and Easter
- Jesus' resurrection and ascension
- The journeys of the apostle Paul

ISBN 978 1 84101 699 3   £8.99
Please visit www.brfonline.org.uk.

Stories for Interactive Assemblies

15 story-based assemblies to get children talking

Nigel Bishop

Collective worship is an ideal time to combine biblical teaching with contemporary storytelling. The 15 stories in this book are all based in the world of the classroom but have their roots in the parables of Jesus. They are designed to stimulate children's thinking and get them talking in the assembly and afterwards in the classroom.

Primary children of all ages will recognise themselves and their classmates in these stories and, even if they do not recognise the original parable, they are invited to relate to its underlying message.

Each story is followed by questions for the assembly or classroom, designed to help the children interact with some of the issues raised, plus suggestions for practical activities, based on different learning styles. Each story also includes:

- A target theme to help direct the teacher towards the main teaching objective
- A prayer or reflection to close the assembly if desired
- Bible references for the original parables
- Information to link the teaching to PSHE/Citizenship and the non-statutory national framework for RE or local SACRE guidelines

ISBN 978 1 84101 465 4   £6.99
Please visit www.brfonline.org.uk.

Barnabas RE Days

Exploring Christianity creatively

A Barnabas RE Day is a full day's visit to your school to bring the Bible to life for primary-aged children through a range of the creative arts. The Barnabas children's ministry team explores the themes 'Whose world?', 'Who is my neighbour?', 'Who am I?', 'What's so special about the Bible?', 'It's not fair', Advent and Christmas, Lent and Easter, and Harvest, using Bible stories and contemporary life illustrations. The themes address many PSHE/Citizenship objectives. For example:

- *Whose world?* What improves or harms our environment; responsibility towards our environment.
- *Who is my neighbour?* Recognising choices; realising that other people have needs; caring; bullying; racism.
- *Who am I?* Recognising similarities and differences between people; feeling positive about ourselves; recognising our worth as individuals; recognising and challenging stereotypes.

The sessions use different creative arts according to the particular skills of the team member undertaking your booking, such as story-telling, music, dance, mime, drama, creative writing or drawing. The material is based on biblical and historical accounts, personal story and shared experience.

The timetable, class groupings and themes are completely flexible and will be organised between you and the Barnabas ministry team to suit your school's needs.

A full-day visit costs just £275, of which £50 is placed down as a non-returnable deposit when booking.

For more information, contact the Barnabas Team Administrator on 01865 319704 or email barnabas@brf.org.uk. You can also visit the website: www.barnabasinschools.org.uk.

What schools have said about Barnabas RE Days:

'A hugely inspirational day which really enthused our children—especially the assembly which appropriately engaged everyone. A request has been made that we have an RE week in school because our RE day was so successful.'

'Staff were unanimous in their view that it was an excellent day.'

'An excellent, informative day. The children enjoyed it immensely and can still remember aspects of their workshops now a month on!'

Barnabas INSET

In addition to publishing resources and running RE Days in school for children, Barnabas also offers INSET sessions for teachers. An INSET session lasts two hours, with the option to run two sessions on one day, and follow-up material is available.

Following discussion with the Barnabas team coordinator and the individual Barnabas team member who will be leading the INSET, a session may combine elements from more than one of the following outlines.

Using Drama in RE
Storytelling and the Bible
Collective Worship and Reflection
Art and Spirituality
Using the Bible with Children

There is also the opportunity to include within the INSET programme an element of 'Quiet Spaces', an enriching and enjoyable time for the staff to be still and reflect on wider questions than day-to-day teaching.

What schools have said about Barnabas INSET:

'Thank you very much for a superb session… it was just what we needed, and I'm sure you realised from the comments as people left that it was very much appreciated by everyone there.'

'When I signed up for your RE INSET day I was looking for an easy day where the children would be inspired by the Bible, and your personality and the way you presented the Bible really inspired me.'

'It was inspirational, demonstrating how to make RE a fun, interactive, experience.'

About
brf:

BRF is a registered charity and also a limited company, and has been in existence since 1922. Through all that we do—producing resources, providing training, working face-to-face with adults and children, and via the web—we work to resource individuals and church communities in their Christian discipleship through the Bible, prayer and worship.

Our Barnabas children's team works with primary schools and churches to help children under 11, and the adults who work with them, to explore Christianity creatively and to bring the Bible alive.

To find out more about BRF and its core activities and ministries, visit:

www.brf.org.uk
www.brfonline.org.uk
www.biblereadingnotes.org.uk
www.barnabasinschools.org.uk
www.barnabasinchurches.org.uk
www.faithinhomes.org.uk
www.messychurch.org.uk
www.foundations21.org.uk

If you have any questions about BRF and our work, please email us at

enquiries@brf.org.uk